Comic Capers THE BASH STREET KIDS

BEANObooks
geddes & grosset

The World's Worst School
Soccer Shocker

© D.C. Thomson & Co., Ltd 2000

Published 2000 by BEANO books geddes & grosset,
an imprint of Children's Leisure Products Limited,
David Dale House, New Lanark ML11 9DJ, Scotland

All rights reserved. No part of this publication may be
reproduced, stored in a retrieval system, or transmitted, in any
form or by any means, electronic, mechanical, photocopying,
recording or otherwise, without the prior permission of the
copyright holder.

ISBN 1 84205 008 7

Printed and bound in Italy

ONE ASSAULT COURSE LATER . . .

NOW IT'S TIME FOR THE ROCKY RUN . . .

ANYTHING I CAN DO, YOU *MUST* DO! FILL YOUR PACKS WITH ROCKS!

A WORD IN YOUR EAR, BENSON! ONE OF YOUR LOT IS MISSING ON THE ASSAULT COURSE!

ONE OF *MY* GUYS HAS NOT RETURNED? IMPOSSIBLE!

WE SHALL SEE!

QUICK, KIDS! BACK TO THE DORMITORY!

WE'LL STUFF OUR PACKS WITH PILLOWS INSTEAD OF ROCKS!

MEANWHILE, OUT ON THE ASSAULT COURSE!

HELP ME, MR BENSON!

SNAP!

KEEP COOL! DON'T PANIC, ELMER!

SNAP!

I'LL PANIC INSTEAD! HELP!

TUT! TUT!

TERROR!

GIVE ME ONE OF YOUR MEDALS, MAN! I NEED THE PIN . . .

MORNING COMES . . .

AH, THE BIG AMERICAN BREAKFAST — BUT YOU GET NONE! YOUR MAN CAME LAST! REMEMBER THE RULES?

♪ OLÉ! OLÉ! OLÉ! WE ARE THE CHAMPS!

I GIVE UP! I'VE APPLIED FOR A POSTING TO THE 7TH DALLAS BROWNIES!

HERE WE GO, KIDS! NEXT STOP IS PARIS!

AIRPORT

TAXIS

PARIS? I LOVE SPAIN!

IDIOT! IT'S IN GERMANY!

NO! IT'S IN GREECE. TWIT!

GEOGRAPHY NEVER WAS THEIR STRONG POINT!

PARIS, FRANCE . . .

THE OPPOSITION

AHA! AHO! HERE COME ZE BASH STREET SCHOOLERS!

CHAPTER THREE

LET BATTLE COMMENCE!

READY TO WELCOME OUR GUESTS? UN, DEUX, TROIS . . .

LIKE OUR *DRESSED* CRAB?

EXCUSE ME PUPILS' LITTLE JOKE! PLEASE ACCEPT ZE CAKE!

I AM GASTON BLANCMANGE, HEADMASTER OF ZE FINEST COOKERY ACADEMY IN THE WORLD!

GULP!

MY CAKES ARE SO GOOD, EVEN I CAN'T RESIST THEM!

BURP! PLEASE ACCEPT MY APOLOGIES! I WAS A LEETLE PECKISH!

YOU QUALIFY ONLY FOR THEE FAMOUS GASTON CHEF HATS IF YOU PRODUCE A DISH THAT WILL ASTOUND ME — BY FOUR O'CLOCK TODAY!

WE NEED FROGS' LEGS FOR THIS RECIPE! I'LL TRY THE LARDER! WAIT HERE!

LE RECIPE BOOK by I. EETALOT

WELL, WE SURE BAKED A CAKE TO IMPRESS OL' GASTON! I'VE EARNED THE GASTON CHEF HAT!

AND WHAT OF SIR WITH HIS NEW FRENCH PUPILS...

IF YOU CAN'T PREPARE THE DISH I DESIRE, BASH STREET WIN THIS ROUND!

AND *YOU* HAVE TO EAT EVERYTHING WE COOK.... OR *WE* WIN!

OH, DEAR!

RIGHT — STARTERS — I'LL HAVE OCTOPUS EYEBALLS IN TADPOLE SAUCE!

THEY'LL NEVER MAKE THAT!

NOT A PROBLEM, SIR!

VOILA!.... AND NOW YOU EAT!

ERK!

I'LL EAT IT! I WON'T LET THE SCHOOL DOWN, GROOH!

RASP!

TUG!

PSST! IT'S SMIFFY, SIR! DON'T PANIC! WE'LL HELP YOU EAT ALL THEY CAN COOK!

NOW, FOR SOUP, I'LL HAVE CREAM OF CAMEL!

SURELY THEY CAN'T DO THAT!

CREAM OF ZE CAMEL, COMING UP!

HOW CAN I BE SURE IT'S CREAM OF CAMEL?

IT'S CREAM OF CAMEL ALL RIGHT!

ULP!

YOU CAN TAKE A BREAK WHILE I THINK UP A MAIN COURSE!

ER . . . MEET YOUR FELLOW CONTESTANTS, CHILDREN. HOW INTERESTING!

THEY'RE THE WORST TRAINED DOGS IN THE COUNTRY!

THAT'S NOTHING — MY LOT ARE THE WORST TRAINED SCHOOLKIDS IN THE WORLD!

NEXT MORNING...

SPECIAL WHISTLE HEARD ONLY BY DOGS AND BASH ST KIDS.

WALKIES!

FETCH THIS, MY LITTLE ROTTWEILERS!

PLOP!!

HEY, CAPTAIN POOP-DECK! YOU'VE TOLD US A SHAGGY DOG STORY — THIS IS FAKE FOOD!

THAT'S RIGHT, MY LITTLE ST BERNARD . . .

. . . IF YOU WANT REAL BREAKFAST, YOU MUST ALL SIT UP AND BEG!

UP HIGHER, TOOTS, HIGHER, FATTY . . .

SCRATCH!

NAUGHTY, FATNESS! COME BACK WITH MY TABLE!

TRIP!

SPLAT!

CRASH!

HE LOOKS LIKE A REAL DOG'S DINNER

YUM!

LISTEN CAREFULLY, TEAM! THIS IS OUR FIRST GAME AND WE HAVE TO GET OFF TO A GOOD START . . . WE'LL PLAY 4-2-4, WITH WILFRID AS SWEEPER, AND WE NEED LOTS OF MAN-MARKING . . . THE OPPOSITION ARE COMFORTABLE ON THE BALL GOING DOWN THE FLANKS . . .

THERE! I'VE FIRED THEM UP FOR THE BATTLE . . .

THE FIRST GAME'S AGAINST DORKSHIRE NURSERY . . . BUT DON'T UNDERESTIMATE THEM . . .

THEY'RE *NURSERY* KIDDIES!

PEEP!!!

THIS IS TOO EASY!

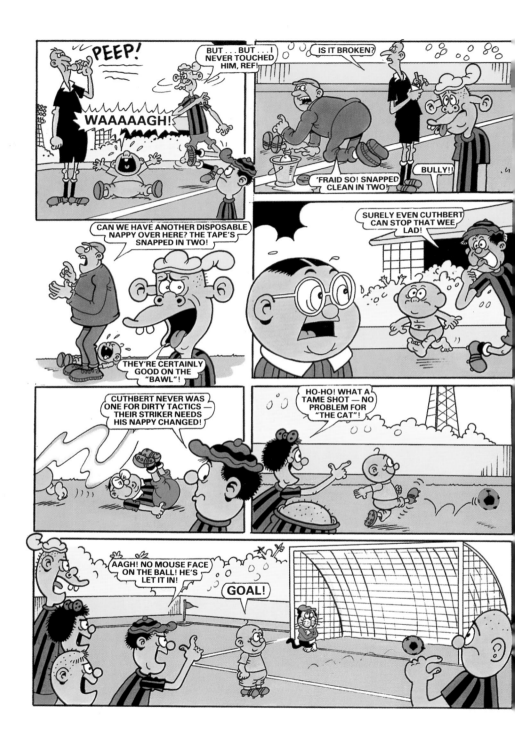

PART TWO — UP FOR THE CUP!

GAZZA THE MENACE HAS INJURED HIS KNEE! THIS COULD DELAY HIS BIG MONEY TRANSFER TO LAZIO ACADEMY — AND WE NEED THE BIG TRANSFER MONEY!

WE'LL BANDAGE IT UP TIGHTLY — THEN NO ONE WILL NOTICE!

I WILL!

PEEP!

THERE, THAT SHOULD DO IT! NO ONE WILL NOTICE IT'S DAMAGED!

WE WATCHA THE GAZZA MENACE TO A-SEE IF HE IS A- FIT.

ISSA WONDERFUL! LOOK AT THEE MUSCLES ON THE GAZZA MENACE — HE REMINDA ME OF A-MAMA!

ISSA FREE KICK!

KEEP THE WALL INTACT! DO LIKE WILFRID'S DOING!

LIKE THIS YOU MEAN?

NO!!!

WHAM!

ME? AN IDIOT

I MEANT 'STAND FIRM', NOT 'DUCK', YOU IDIOT!

WE NOT A-SEE TOO MANY OF THEE GASSA DRIBBLING SKILLS! IS A-HE A-FIT OR A-NOT? EH?

TIME FOR ACTION! HOLD TIGHT, DENNIS!

SPINNN...

YIKES!!

GOAL!!

BLIP!

WHATA SKILLS! HE ISSA MAGNIFICO! QUICK! WE SIGN-A HEEM AT ONCE!!

WEAR THIS TO MASK THE PAIN!

THROB!

SIGN A-HERE, MA BOY! I TAKE YOU HOME TO MAMA.

£

CONTRACT

FOOTBALL CLUB

QUICK! LET'S GO BEFORE HE TAKES OFF THE DARK SPECS!

SPORTS SHOP

NOW WE CAN BUY NEW STRIPS FOR THE *BIG* MATCH!

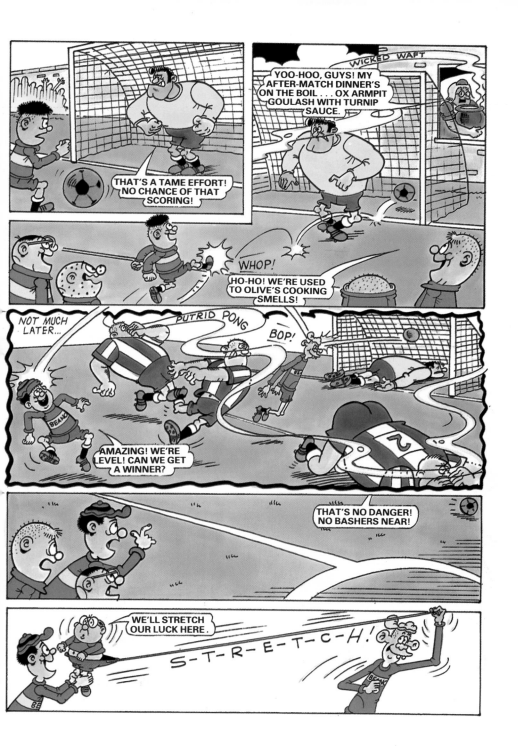